Reading The Stars

Ashley Nemer & Stacy A. Moran

Reading The Stars

ISBN-13: 978-1-941194-06-5

ISBN-10: 1-941194-06-0

A product of the
Art of Safkhet
Published September 2015

Other Works By

Maverick Touch: The Cat by Ashley Nemer

Maverick Touch: The Highway by Ashley Nemer

Maverick Touch: The Adventure by Ashley Nemer

Blood Purple by Ashley Nemer

Blood Yellow by Ashley Nemer

Blood Green by Ashley Nemer

Blood White by Ashley Nemer

Special Assignment by Niki Becker

Bud's Christmas Wish by Ashley Nemer

Bud's Christmas Miracle by Ashley Nemer

Under the Moonlight: A Mermaid's Tale by Ashley Nemer

The Café (Temptation Tuesday) by Niki Becker

After Hours (Temptation Tuesday) by Anabella Adrian

Fantasy Cruise (Temptation Tuesday) by Niki Becker

The Backyard (Temptation Tuesday) by Niki Becker

Pleasured Pleasantries (Temptation Tuesday) by Nasira Thomas

The Last Day (Temptation Tuesday) by Anabella Adrian

Sekhmet's Revenge Volume One through Four by Ashley Nemer
& Stacy A. Moran

STARLIGHT SHIMMERING
BY
ASHLEY NEMER

They Say

They say it's darkest before the dawn but not when dawn will come

They tell me things will get better but give me no timeframe

They tell me I am wrong but offer no solution

They tell me....

Where are you my angel?

Where are you my strength?

Where are you my spirit?

They tell me you're near but give me no sight

They tell me you're looking down from up above, but I cannot see

They tell me in the end I was justified, but I feel so little

They tell me

I call to you my angel

I call to you my strength

Give me freedom from this hell

Give me peace from with in

Darkness

I walk, but I hear no sound. I listen but see no one around. Do I continue traveling maintaining hope? Do I turn around and hide?

I walk but sense nothing. I listen but feel numb. Why have others forsaken me? Why am I always surprised?

I walk and feel wetness. I listen and hear my cries. Always alone and isolated. Always pushed to the side.

Darkness Awaits me, Darkness scares me. Darkness is my life.

If I die young

She knew better than to go downstairs alone feeling like she feels. This always happens when she is left alone with her thoughts. She tries to fight the urges to grab the blade. She knows how the cool metal feels on her skin. She remembers that night when she had the tip pressed into her vein, the red droplets staining her skin.

She stands in the doorframe bracing the wood, her fingers clinging to the grooves in the two by four edgings. The handle's wood coloring she eyes knowing how good the weight feels in her palm. She tries to move her feet forward but stays remaining in the same spot. Why can't she move? Why can't she just end the pain she is feeling? Knowing she can't remain how she is she has to find another way to carry this out. What is the point in living if she is dead inside? She can't feel anymore, she is numb to the pain and sorrow. She's translucent, as a shade, people know she is there but can't see her for what she is. She screams for help and no one hears the words she says.

All she wants is someone to love her. Someone to hold her when she cries, laugh with her when she's happy and experience life with her. Hasn't she fought hard enough for the shred of happiness?

She watches her life go bye in a haze; she sees people around her but doesn't know where they come from. She reaches out for her dreams, but they are unattainable. She doesn't have the courage to do what is necessary to achieve them. How can she turn her back on her life and fight for her hearts desires?

She backs up away from the kitchen and moves towards the front door. She knows what is outside this house. She knows what she can use to end her existence. She grabs the handle and turns the cool brass knob. Opening the door to the outside land, she crosses the threshold and stands on her porch. She stares out into the tree line, how beautiful the fall leaves look swaying in the wind. She savors this last image; it's what she will be taking to the grave.

Right foot. Left foot. Stepping off of the stairs and into the field closing her eyes and let the flames start at her feet. Working their way up her legs, then pelvis, torso then finally skull her body fully engulfed in the fire she feel her soul start to drift away as she screams in agony....

The pain taking her to an ecstasy she's never experienced.

Blackness

The clouds cover my home shielding out the light
The winds knock on the door demanding entrance

Lights flicker off and on while powers fading fast
What allows me to breathe starts to suffocate
What allows my freedom starts to enslave
My demise feels certain, my death eminent

The creeping feeling up my spine tingles through my body
The blade about to make its stab
Earth shaking, the house quaking
Whatever shall I do?
Whatever shall I face?

Pain slicing through me, blood starts to flow
The Cries for help useless
The Cries for forgiveness gone
Cries Cries Cries ....I cry for everyone

I've Died

I cry and no one is there to hold me
I bleed and no one is there to fix
I weep for what I'm losing
I die a little each day

I scream, but no one hears the words I say
I fight, but no one is there to punch back
I repeat myself, but no one seems to get it
I die a little each day

They see right through me as though I'm a figment
They treat me as if I'm second-class
They hear what they want not what I mean
They kill me a little each day

They watch me drift apart and don't stop
They chain down my desires and hopes
They beat me with their words
They kill me a little each day

I'll just give in to their words
I'll give in to their beatings…
I give.

Lightning

The blackness in life chases at your spirits
It weakens the heart

The light in dark times draws you in
But can it save your soul

The banshees bellow out your name
They seduce you with fear

The lightning strikes
The thunder cracks
The roaring fear takes you whole

So pray for your sins
Ask for forgiveness

Pray for the ones you love
Will you see them at Heaven's Gate?

Review the lessons
Study the test
Show your Self to the world

Wreckage

You pull me from the wreckage but aren't you the one to cause it…
You wrap me in your arms and tell me it will be okay but aren't you
the one who made me cry…
You claim it's for my own good, you claim it's for the best…
Why does your opinion matter?
Why do your words cut?
Why is your approval important
You pull me up from the fall but aren't you the one who keeps
pushing
You wrap yourself in my life yet you continuously tell me I'm wrong
You claim you know best, you claim you're the end all be all
Why can't I tell you to go to hell?
Why can't I stand up for myself?
Maybe It's time I start

Forever you are MINE

Lying in bed at night I think of you, the long brown hair that flows
across your back. The way you used to hold me when we were
younger. The way we stole quiet glances across the room. The way
our hands touched, our skin, how it tingled. The taste of your blood
inside me. How you melted my heart. How you teased my senses.
Forever you are MINE

Your laugh when I tickled you. Your tears when you're sad. The way
you sank your teeth into me. The way your scent filled me. Nothing
about you is replaceable. Nothing about you should change.
Forever you are MINE

Our lives have grown apart, but somehow we always come back.
Drawn to you in my dreams and heart. Forever our souls are one.
You are my laughter. You are my joy.
Forever you are MINE

Immortal Love

The Immortal Love runs deep in your veins
It's there to warm your body when the chill passes by
The Immortal Love fuels your soul
It provides your energy for life
The Immortal Love drives away the pain
It protects you from your fears
The Immortal Love strengthens the memories you cherish
It protects the happiness when you're sad
The Immortal Love combines all that is pure and holy
It is THE gift of the gods

Memories

I remember the way you used to touch my hair and how your fingers would linger at the pull. I remember the way you would kiss my neck and how your tongue danced across my skin. I remember how you held me, keeping me warm and safe. I remember how you made me laugh, being the joys of my day. I remember how you and I would spend hours talking, our ramblings lasting days.

I remember how you held me when I cried, rocking me to sleep. I remember the way you would kiss me, our tongues and lips touching each other. I remember the way we were. I remember the times we had. I remember.

No day will come that my mind will forget. No night will pass that I don't wish. No morning will start that I don't remember. Our Love, Our Friendship, our Past.

So here is to us and the paths we make. Here is to the future, the untold fate. Here is to the present, the rough journey ahead. Here is to us, because deep down inside, we are still the same.

Your Rainbow

You travel through life in colors of wonderment
You look for those greener places
You travel through life in colors of light
The pinks and yellows brightening your day
You travel through life in the colors of noble
Blues and reds follow in your path
You travel through life in the colors of a rainbow
Skiing through the good times and the bad

Fear not for at the end there is salvation
The pot of gold to greet your needs
Fear not for at the end there is happiness
The pot of life full of memories past
Fear not at the end there is your image
The pot of life over spilling with your goodness

You travel through life in the colors of a rainbow
And every day will be a new surprise

A Dog's Loyalty

You make us smile when opening the door to see your face
You were there for us when we were sick always laying by our side
You're my little protector, saving me from the bee when I couldn't
move

You hid in our bed when we weren't home, but we always knew
You cry when it rains and whimper at the thunder even though most
humans are scared of you

You hate the ocean when the tides chase you along the shore and all
we wanted to do was play
You love the flies and chasing them about attacking them mid air
You're the best friend no one can live without loyal till the end

You hide in our cloths and take our sheets
You were the best we could have had
All the things a pet can be, you were
And now my heart breaks at the loss of you

My Grandpa, My Hero, My Inspiration

I lay here at night listening to you breathe. Your hands reach out, I hold and cry

I lay here at night listening to your heart. Your legs kick and move all through the night

I lay here at night remembering the Irish tales. Your mind wandering the worlds. Looking for rest

I lay here at night and cry because I will always remember

I will remember to pray for the Irish I will remember the magic garage door dance I will remember the sleigh rides I will remember the Spades game I will remember the advice I will remember the laughs

My life has been saturated with your love

My world filled with your joy

You make me want to be a better person You make me want to live So here is to the Irish that you love To the Jayhawk that you are To the lawyer who inspires To the father and grandfather beloved

May God bless you and keep you safe in my heart May God hear your inner prayers May God keep you with us just a little longer

My love for you overflows My love for you soars My love for you will never be forgotten

My Grandpa, My Hero, My Inspiration

Ghostly Love

The best kinds of friend to have are the ones you can't see but know
they're there

The ones who float around and hold your hand even if you don't
realize it

They always listen and don't judge

Sometimes you talk and don't even realize they are listening

The best kinds of friend to have are Ghost

The Winds

The winds of change bring forth a new spirit, one that doesn't
include you

The winds of change bring forth a new light, one that exposes you
for what you are

The winds of change bring forth a new hope that that teaches
patience and respect

The winds of change bring forth a new desire, one that focuses on
peace, not strife

The winds of change bring forth a new thought, one that fills you
with love, not anger

The winds of change bring forth a new appreciation, the kind that
actually live your life

The winds of change bring forth a new friendship, one based on
equality and kindness

The winds of change bring forth a new spirit, one that doesn't
include you

The Sun

The Sun rises to an open plane, vast in the distance, covered in color.
Down the path the Sun travels, touching it all, providing warmth.
Over the mountaintops and through the valley's it moves west,
searching for a home. The Angels and Saints up above watch with
pleasure as the Sun nourishes all that comes in contact with it.
The Sun, our Sun, the provider of life, the provider of all.
Through its travels, it sees many a things.
It experiences the joy of creation.
The Sun comes to us daily and casts a shadow on any doubt of the
love it possesses for us.
The Sun is a force like no other, showing no weakness
The Sun will conquer all obstacles and fights for what's right
The Sun, nothing stronger, nothing better.
We each possess our own Sun. Our Light, Our Spirit, Our Strength
My Sun lives in my heart where it's safe and warm
My Sun, fought for justice, protected the weak, loved his family and
country.
My Sun was a man like no other.
My Sun, will burn all my life, and help guide me along my travels.
My Sun, My Grandpa, My strength

Lost

The days of saints are lost
The time for faith passed us up
All that's left is loneliness

The chance for survival dismal
The odds of winning slim
All that's left is loneliness

You ask what's going on
You pretend like you care
You're just a shell of person

You wonder why I'm gone
You wonder where we split
You're as lost as me

So travel till the day meets night
Travel all the morning light
Travel till you can't go any further
Travel till the ends in sight

Angel in Heaven

My Ellie rests on a cloud above where the angels play and everything's okay

My Ellie laughs and runs in the Heavens fields of flowers and trees

My Ellie watches as life goes on what the world would have been like with her here

My Ellie rests on a cloud above where the angels play and everything's okay

My Ellie sings the song of the wind, I hear her when the trees sway

My Ellie sees me in my dreams where we are safely away from death and harm

My Ellie rests on a cloud above where the angels play and everything's okay

My Ellie talks to me in whispers only heard by a mother

My Ellie lights up my world when she is near

My Ellie will always be in my heart

A Father's Love

A father's love knows no limits of time and space; he's there for his children always.

He's there to hold you at birth wrap you safely in blankets always protecting you.

A fathers love is the one thing you can count on when you need to cry and feel comfort.

He teaches you to pray at night, he teaches you to write and sing.
A father's love is everlasting. No barriers will ever keep it out.
He coaches your sports, teaches you to swim, and helps you build character and strength.

A father's love can engulf you when in sorrow; fill you with laughter and joy.

He sees you walk across the stage; achieving the degree he helped support.

A father's love means the world to you, forever being in your heart and soul.

He walks you down the aisle and kisses your cheek and gives you away, fighting back the tears.

A father's love is unbreakable, not even death can squash the feelings.

He holds your hand as life hits you hard, helping you stand and walk through the fires of life.

A father's love is everything. Not anything money can buy.
He's your Idol, your hero, your rock. He's Your Father.

True Love

I watch from a distance as you lay in your bed. I watch your chest rise and lower with your breaths. You're a hero to many, and a great man of your time. I walked down the aisle with you and exchanged a ring. I took your name and bore your children. I traveled my life with you at my side.

I watch as I move beside you, our last journey together. Your laugh and smile echoing in the room. You're the man of my heart the keeper of my soul. For all the times, we cried and laughed are drowning out the pain and sorrow. You helped me down the steps of life and will be there when I pass. Your hand will once again reach out for mine, down the aisle that is life.

I'll love you forever and carry you in my heart. Our deepest secrets our brightest lights, together they will keep me whole until I join you in the ever more.

Warrior's Adventure

Out of the flames, we are reborn onto a new path of greatness
Our pointed daggers of steal lead our way through the shadows
The internal light burns bright inside our new bodies
Flames ignite our deepest desires sending images of heat and power
through our minds

Life has changed and our old existence no longer of importance
Will our bags be ready for our new journey?
Will our spirits live up to the challenge?

The Gods of Thunder crackle displaying their strength
The lives invested in their steps following in tune
The Queens of existence push through the crowds never being
derailed

The hotel's waiting
The end's in the distance
All that's left…
Is her Warrior's Adventure

Fire

Up through the darkness you shine
Through the air you travel
Around the world you kill

Burn
Burn
Burn

Destroy the life within
Suffocate the air
Become the end

Burn
Burn
Burn

You Don't

You don't deserve me
You don't deserve my love
You don't deserve my kindness
You don't deserve my tears
You don't deserve me

I'm Tired, I'm Worn, I'm Weathered

I'm tired, I'm worn, I'm weathered...
I have nothing left to give - I have nothing left for life

I'm tired, I'm worn, I'm weathered...
Winds whip around me - slicing through my skin

I'm tired, I'm worn, I'm weathered...
Tears run down my cheeks - anger settled under my skin

I'm tired, I'm worn, I'm weathered...
You've broken me down to nothing - you've taken me for all I've had

I'm tired, I'm worn, I'm weathered...

What Started in the Past Has Grown

What started in the past has grown
Love's devotion – Love's strong hold
The first walk along the life's road
Love's devotion – Love's strong hold

The dark of your skin draws me in
The warmth of your smile holds me there
Your hands so rough
Your hearts so large

Your words of wisdom always play in my head
Your laughter, your love, your everything wraps inside our hearts

What we have in the future no one knows
Where our paths cross, only God knows
Why our lives keep falling together
One of the World's mysteries…left to be told

The Way I Fell In Love With You….

There is a smile on my face, a big one, one that cannot be removed if anyone tried. You might ask why, you might look at me and think I'm on cloud 9. Well, here is your reason why…

6 years ago this weekend I said I do, I said I'd love you till my dying day
6 years ago this weekend I said I do, I said I'd cherish you above all others
6 years ago this weekend I said I do, I said I'd stick it through with you
6 years ago this weekend I said I do, I said I love you.

There is a smile on my face, a big one, one that cannot be removed if anyone tried. You might ask why, you might look at me and think I'm on cloud 9. Well, here is your reason why…
8 ½ years ago you gave me the giggles, you made my heart flutter and my stomach tumble
8 ½ years ago you gave me the giggles, you made me twirl, smile, and sing
8 ½ years ago you gave me the giggles, you made my eyes open and see the light
8 ½ years ago you gave me the giggles, you made me fall in love.

There is a smile on my face, a big one, one that cannot be removed if anyone tried. You might ask why, you might look at me and think I'm on cloud 9. Well, here is your reason why…
You lie on the couch and read with me
You laugh with me in the car
You hold me during the scary parts
You pour cold water on me in the worst spots!
You sing me songs
You draw me pictures
You bring me love like no others

There is a smile on my face, a big one, one that cannot be removed if anyone tried. And it is all because of you…

Ashley Nemer & Stacy A. Moran

I Want to Be the Reason You Wake Up

I want to be the reason you wake up

I want to be the reason you smile

I want to be the reason you strive for more

I want to be the reason you survive

I want to be the reason you act out

I want to be the reason you exist

I want to be....

Take Away My Hurt, Take Away My Pain

Take away my hurt, take away my pain
Take away the sorrow that fills my heart
Take away my hurt, take away my pain
Take away the plague that devours my soul
Take away my hurt, take away my pain
Take away the destruction that never stops ending
Take away my hurt, take away my pain
Take me away

I'll Be

I'll be there when the world stops spinning
I'll be there when the evil hits.
I'll be there when the fog lifts
I'll be there when the terror stops reigning

The clouds will part and the sun will shine
The earth will spin and wash away the grime
The love will flow in the ever more
The heart will beat up until death's door

I'll be there when you're ready
I'll be there when you're home
I'll be there when you're wanting
I'll be there when you're needing

The love of family will never break
The laughter and tears always in our wake
The smiles and good times forever a memory
The joyous gladness forever our legacy

I'll be there when you're ready
I'll be there open and waiting.

Sand

Sand crinkles between my toes....waves wash over my skin
The thoughts vanish from my body as newness starts to set in

Sand crinkles between my toes....dead skin and memories leave
making room for the new adventures to fill the spaces in my mind
body and soul

Sand crinkles between my toes....walking along the shore, the sun
beating down on my back, filling my skin with nourishment and color

Sand crinkles between my toes....sounds of heaven play in my ears as
each step moves closer and closer down the new journey and path

Sand crinkles between my toes....for how long.....nobody knows...

2-2

I sat there waiting and you were late.
I sat there waiting and thought you changed your mind.
I sat there waiting impatient and nervous.
I sat there waiting.....

You showed up before I left
You saved me from my hell
You made me see how special I was
You made me feel whole

I sat there waiting for a lifetime
I sat there watching you pass us by
I sat there still and lonely
I sat there waiting.....

You never really left me
You never really will
You never really understood
You never really will

I sat there waiting and you found me
I sat there hoping you would come
You make promises never to leave me
You make promises that I hold true

Years later you will still be there
Years later I will be waiting
Years later we can be whole

You Break Me

You break me
You burn me
You hurt me
You push me

I crumble I cry I survive

You destroy me
You ignite me
You sever me
You punish me

I rebuild I move forward I survive

I pull the pieces together
I grow a new
I am stronger
I fight back

I rebuild I move forward I survive

Just For a Moment

The sounds of the clock behind me click with every heart beat
The time passing by freezes, unable to move, unable to continue
My eyes look to the knife on the desk; they close and push back the
tears
The grandfather clock in the other room dings at the stroke of seven
The world stops short as the blade slices through my skin
The warm blood runs down my wrist, across my palm and on the
white carpet
The knife falls to the floor, the chair behind me becomes my savior,
keeping me off the ground
Where were you to save me this time?
Where were you to free me from these chains?
Where were you to bring me the light and show me how it could be?
Where were you this day?
The numbness starts to take over my hand, working its way up my
arm
I'm cold scared and alone…
Just for a moment I'll close my eyes…rest them for this day
Maybe tomorrow I can wake up and this will all be a dream
Salvation will be here and the sun will warm me, death will be just a
dream

The Soulless Survival

Racing through the heavens, nothing left to see
Chasing my past, nothing left to forgive
Running through the streets, nothing left to visit

Leaving my home, full of peace and warmth
Packing for a trip that I'll never get to finish
Loving the life I had even if it was doomed

Fighting for the truth when nothing is making sense
Fighting for the second chance to right my wrongs
Fighting for the love that I am leaving behind

Meeting the devil and paying my dues
Bargaining for my last ride
Making me see the errors of my ways

Giving up the one I truly loved
Giving up the one I cherished
Giving up the one I need

Existing, existing without my soul,
Along the streets paved in heartache,
Ignoring the remaining few

Weathering It

We weather the storms and come out ahead
We hold each other and cry in the rain

Thunder cracks and lightning strikes
The sound of terror rippling through the night

Earth under our feet begins to quake
Everything around us starts to shake

Our world toppled over
Our lives a mess

Always together
Always unruffled

We weather the storms and come out ahead
We hold each other and cry in the rain

Never be scared of what the future holds
Because wherever we end up, we'll always have each other

One Year Ago

You smiled my way, one year ago
You held my hand and gave me strength, one year ago
You laughed at my joke, one year ago
Your heart still beat, one year ago

We've laid you to rest
We've shed our tears
We've held you close
We've faced our fears

Your food I made
Your mouth I fed
Your forehead I kissed
Your hugs I accepted

One year ago you left us
One year ago you flew
One year ago seems like forever
One year ago … it's still new

My Heart Feels Heavy

My eye lids still full of tears
My life forever changed
My foundation forever shaken

Your voice is still in my head
Your warmth still surrounds me
Your life force never left my realm
Your lessons still inside my head

Are you looking down on us?
Are you pleased with what you see?
Are you enjoying the gates of heaven?
Are you shuffling your deck of cards?

One year ago you left us
One year ago you flew
One year ago you went home
One year ago … It's still new

The Family I Wish I Knew

Through random acts of life, you're gone
Through miracles of God you'll live on in us

Through random acts of life, we're family
Through miracles of God, you'll live on in friends

Through random acts of life, you're now home
Through miracles of God, you'll live on

Though we didn't speak as much as either of us wanted
We're family

Though we didn't see each other as much, as either of us hoped
We're family

Though we didn't know each other as much a cousins should
We're family

Now you're up with the Angels
Now you're up with the Father
Now you're up with our Relatives
Now you're up

May God hold you in his palms
May God show you the lives you touched
May God bless you with life everlasting

The Family I Wish I Knew - was you

Near and Far

Though far away we're always near in thought
Though far away we're always near with love
Though far away we're always near in spirit
Though far away we're always near with love
Life's puzzles always have rough edges
Life's puzzles always end up complete
Life's puzzles always travel in shades of colors
Life's puzzles always bring us close
Looking through you we see our future
Looking through you we see our past
Looking through you we see our potential
Looking through you we see our fate
Near and far our desires travel
Near and far our wishes roam
Near and far our deepest desires are born
Near and far our life forms
Although life kept us apart, we found our way back
The mysteries of faith helped to guide our way
And together we'll always be stronger when you're near and I'm far

I Dream of You...

I dream of you, but I can't see your face
I know your scent, but I've never smelled your skin
You're in my dreams and in my heart ... but I've never met you
You're the one I dream of at night, your name on the tip of my
tongue
Everything I crave is you
Everything I need is beyond my reach

I dream of you, but I can't see your face
I know your scent, but I've never smelled your skin
Ten fingers and ten toes I know are there
I just won't ever feel lying upon my skin

Everything I crave is you
Everything I need is beyond my reach
You are a part of my heart and soul
You are my everything
The child I've never known

Sun Moon and Stars

Lying in the grass and looking up above
The Sun shines back brightly saying hello

Sailing at night looking for directions
The Stars up above guild the path

Hearing the howl of the dogs at night
Knowing the Moon is high up in the sky

Simple things bring joys
Simple things bring sorrow
Simple things come and go

But only three things promise to remain

The Sun
The Moon
And The Stars

LOST IN THE STARS
BY
STACY A. MORAN

Fairy Tales

A time for fairy tales
From my book of life
I'll tell you of dreams
I'll tell you of life's mysteries
Where life is free of stress
Where love stories will unfold
Of white lions and tigers
And where the unicorns roam
As your heart opens
You'll see the beauty
The magic that can be found
In lands where myths begin
Dragons roam with fiery breath
We turn another page
Fairies twinkle in the dark
In the sky, there are witches on broomsticks
Princesses sing and dance
Elves hide in the fields
Dwelling where rainbows meet the grass
Rain sprinkles like fairy dust
Kissing your cheek gently
Like whispers in the dark

My Loves

My loves from my womb

Whose eyes would they of had
Crystal blue like the sky above or dark as the blackest night

The joy of yesterday

Is the heartbreak today
Gone is the hope for tomorrow

My flesh and soul I would offer
Forever, I would give up
To see their eyes shine or to touch their little cheeks

My loves from my womb
Whose eyes would they of had
Crystal blue like the sky above or dark as the blackest night

Ashley Nemer & Stacy A. Moran

Darkness

My soul seems to live in darkness

Darkness, where my passion thrives
Like a ravenous beast
Waiting to devour my love

My soul hides anticipating

Darkness, where my hunger lurks
Like an eager vulture
Waiting to tear at the decay of my love

My soul drains my sanity

Darkness, where my desire searches
Like a wolf prowling the night
Waiting to consume the strength of my love

My soul seems to live in darkness

This is where it thrives, where it lurks, and where it searches…

Shh...

Shh my angel, close your sleepy eyes

Feel the love you hold inside
Trust my voice and let it be your guide

Dreams will come feel them hidden deep
Blankets of love cover you in warmth

Keep my baby safe until morning rise
Shh my angel, close your sleepy eyes

Only Once

Only once have I felt his touch
His warm breath against my skin

Only once have I felt his love
His tender heart beating against mine

Forever trapped in darkness and despair
My breath lost in hopelessness

Forever longing only to be with him again
My breath held waiting

Only once have I felt his touch

Haunted

ALONE in this hell, my hell…

The night calls to me, it draws me in close
Tears slide down my frozen cheek
All the memories of the past flood my soul
What you did, I could not walk away unscathed
Even now after all these years
I lose another piece of myself at the thought of you

ALONE in this hell, my hell…

I am frozen, your words still linger inside my brain
The more I try to forget the more you consume me
Anger mixed with hurt and the pain mingled with rage
Your presence surrounds me, but you are not here
You hide in my memories, hammering in my head
Even through your death, I remain haunted

ALONE in this hell, my hell…

Ashley Nemer & Stacy A. Moran

In the Middle of the Night

The middle of the night was when the raven took her flight

With a flash and clap of thunder – she prayed for time to freeze
She was just another victim in their eyes
Advancing with blade gleaming, she was done praying
She hardly spared him a glance as he cowered in the corner
The sound of his heart beating pounded in her ear
His eyes dark infused with fear
With a horrid sneer, anger rose and filled her soul
Her heart turned black as she sliced through flesh
She allowed the monster to surface and pushed back her tears

The middle of the night was when the raven took her flight

Vengeance

Radiant heat churns in the pit of her core

Escalating into waves that washed over her
Her mind is a tumultuous frenzy of ravenous ponderings
Her deep longing to rain down due punishment

Every vibrant vision comes to life inside her
Yearning to feel their pain, to bear down mercilessly
She would show no compassion

Her mouth curved into a smile as each scene played in her mind
Each scene becoming, more gruesome than the last
To watch as they turn on each other

They are oblivious to their own concocted doom
She will savor every second as their lives fade away into oblivion
The satisfaction will quell her demons inside

Yet this vengeance will be her own demise

Radiant heat churns in the pit of her core

She Was...

She was unleashed
To reign evil, everywhere she went
Bringing chaos to society

She was awakened
To give death, bloodily and brutally
With no mercy

She was summoned
To reign over the Gods
Shedding their blood

She was created
To care for no one
Only the evil flowing through her veins

She was awakened
To defeat Death
For he is her slave

Farewell

Farewell, my child of my love
Was my hope too much?

The months of cradling you in my womb
The heart break of never holding you

Should I seek revenge for this sin?
Should I envy those with a better fate?

Farewell, my child of my love
Was my hope too much?

Whispers in the Dark

You are like whispers in the dark
A soft kiss tickling my skin
You are like the rain tapping at my window
A persistent dance against my soul

You are like whispers in the dark
The touch of your breath caressing my cheek
You are like the rain tapping at my window
The feel of your wet skin sliding against my body

You are like whispers in the dark
A gentle love, filling my heart

Just an Echo

Just an echo in the darkness
The wind whispers across my cheek
A shadow catches my eye
I think I feel your breath on my neck
Is that you purring in my ear?
Are you really here or
Just an echo in the darkness?
I wake up drenched in tears, alone
Every night, I spend without you
Crumbles my soul
My body grows so lonely, longing for your touch
I feel your lips on mine
My fingers in your hair
But this isn't real, it's
Just an echo in the darkness

Undeniable

Undeniable ladies follow
Not knowing the danger they seek
Swaying hips and seductive smiles
Dusked with svelte unashamed hope

Undeniable ladies follow
Not knowing the danger they seek
Little girls marching to love
Feeding their dreams, with your lips

Undeniable ladies follow
Not knowing the danger they seek
Immense pleasure their hope
Blindly dancing into love, they will not find

Undeniable ladies follow
Not knowing the DEATH they seek

Perfection

I don't know where it started
I don't know where it will end

I want to never forget every touch, every taste
The feel of your hand on the small of my back

The taste of your sweet kiss
I want to remember every sound, every sight

The soft purrs you breathe in my ear
The sight of you hovering over me

I want to never forget the perfection of it all

Surrounded by Rain

Surrounded by rain in the midnight hour
The darkness and solitude of the quiet rain
Reminding me again of your power
The steady pour will never wash your sins clean

Surrounded by the rain in the midnight hour
Drowning in the silence but swimming in the storm

Surrounded by the rain in the midnight hour
The light of the moon and the wild rain
Reminding me again of my power
The thunderstorm will never hide your sins

Surrounded by the rain in the midnight hour
Drowning in the silence but swimming in the storm

When I am with you

When I am with you
I don't remember the constraints
The betrayal, the dread

When I am with you
I don't remember the darkness
The loneliness, the emptiness

When I am with you
I don't remember the fear
The anger, the revenge

When I am with you
I just have one thought lingering
I am just your love

Regrets...

I believed you were sent from another world
There has never been anyone like you

You stole my heart when we first met
I fell in love instantly

Only you could break down my walls
When I needed you… you were always there

No matter our distance
My love for you remained

I knew forever we would be one
My life began to crumble when you told me

I cried not believing it was true
When you needed me…I regret I was not like you

My heart longed for you, but my feet remained frozen
I regret that only from phone lines I was there in the end

As You Emerge

As you emerge you fill my soul
My soul is alive again in your eyes
As you emerge you fill my heart
My heart beats again in your arms
As you emerge you fill my arms
My life is in your arms as you emerge

Insatiable

The insatiable need comes to attack you
It never ceases in its attempt to destroy
But you hold it close and gently nurse from it
So it stays forever because the need is your only way to survive
This is the one thing that has never betrayed you
Oh but you want it gone
You want to kill the need and the hunger
But the need is ravenous
It nurtures you and like a child afraid of losing its mother
You grab it and hold it tight
Even though it suffocates you
You can't let it go
You are its child, part of its flesh and bone
You live knowing you created your own nightmare
The monster you cling to is you
The voracious need you created is you
The insatiable need comes to attack you
It never ceases in its attempt to destroy

Solitude

In your solitude, the silence keeps you safe
You are at peace but only for the moment

It is already fading, into its lifeless shell

You are trapped in your own hell

You make up a fairy tales, to hide the pain

But your soul has already shriveled up in distain

Inside you, fire burns and anger churns

In your solitude, the silence keeps you safe
You are at peace but only for the moment

Find Me...

Find me in the night, like the sultry dance of rain falling from the
blackened sky

Look for me in the dark where our candle-less love began
Search for me under the moon's glow, seeking shelter in your
arms

Find me naked and wrap me in your strong arms, lay in my love
Calm the waves, I swim into, become the sea in my dreams

Show me the light of the morning sky, I promise to let your love
encompass my heart

Just find me in the night...

Searching

He has gone hunting, searching
For a hope and a vision

I love this man who has gone searching
His nose smells it, his bones know the feel of it
His mind full of instinct and admiration.
What he misses, he hunts, as I watch him from my internal hell

I love this man who has gone hunting
He treads the surf and rides the ocean blue
Searching for a vision
He surfs the waves... like the hips of a woman he had once loved

Ashley Nemer & Stacy A. Moran

The Cloud

The cloud brings showers for the thirsty flowers
Flourishing the seas and the streams
Shading the light from the trees
Allowing their day time dreams
Dancing across the sky, flirting with the sun
Wields the thrash of the heavy hail
Turning to snow on the mountains below
Laughing again as the clouds pass through the thunderous storms.
While we sleep in the mist of the whistling breeze
The clouds shape and shift in gentle motion
To dance once again the next time there is a howling wind

Tranquil Sky

Tranquility of the painted sky
A wondrous cloud dances by

The blue of the canvas begins to fade
Into a pallet of a glorious shade

Sitting in a lazy chair
A gust of traveling fresh air

Tranquility of the painted sky
A wondrous cloud dances by

Eternal Sleep

Last night, where ruins plague the land
I walked through the desert sand

The moon's luminous glow danced over relics left in decay
The path traveled led to their pillared dismay

Fallen pharaohs who now lay in a heap
Their myths and legends in an eternal sleep

Last night, where ruins plague the land
I walked through the desert sand

Until the Next Kiss

Violently raging in a world of madness
Finding our release through pains of flesh
Night after night filled with passionate misery
Violating each other with each lustful touch
Sadness and hatred spilling from our souls
The extremity of our passion contorted with trepidation
Coldness in our hearts seduced shelter in each other's arms
Exhausted and fulfilled, lost in our embrace
Two bodies finally find peace
Satisfied smiles planted firmly on their lips
Each seeking rest until it's time for their next kiss.

Do You Not?

Do you not hear?
Should I write it all down?
But would you even read it?
I know the fear always plugged up your ears.
With so many problems, how will we survive?
Do you not see?
Should I read it for you?
But would you even listen?
I know the hurt and pain always blinds your vision.
With so many excuses, how will we survive?
Do you not speak?
Should I listen to you?
But would you even talk?
I know the emotions will choke your words.
With so many reasons, how will we survive?
Do you not hear? Unplug our ears...
Do you not see? Open our eyes...
Do you not speak? Spit out our words...
Take a deep breath...
Stop pretending to be flawless...
There is something wrong and it's okay...

A Mother's Love

A face with bright blue eyes and ruby red lips is on my mind
Warm hugs, a kiss on the cheek and a pat of the hand, is on my
mind
Kind words spoken with the gentlest voice is on my mind
How your smile remained during the months of pain, is on my
mind
The last battle you could not fight is on my mind
Your fight to stay with us is on my mind
You must have known your time was soon, is on my mind
The tears that were shed and the goodbyes that were said is on my
mind
In the end how I missed so much, is on my mind
Trying to understand, is on my mind
Your beauty and grace are on my mind
The love you shared is on my mind

A mother's love is on my mind...

Ashley Nemer & Stacy A. Moran

Through All the Years

Through all the years, we stood side by side
Always true friends till the end

Or so I thought…

All of life's changes, I was there
Knowing one day you would do the same

Or so I thought…

A shoulder to cry on when times were rough
The time would always be made

Or so I thought…

Supporting all our hopes and dreams
Backing each other through it all

Or so I thought…

Through all the years, we stood side by side
Always true friends till the end

Maybe It Is...

Maybe it is my destiny, the fate within
That must be the reason why
I have this desperate desire, this frantic longing

Or is it the inward dread of it all being nothing?
Why does my purpose begin and end with destruction?
Is it heaven that mingles within my soul?
Or is it the hell that reigns high inside my heart?
Could you live an eternity without annihilation?

Maybe it is my destiny, the fate within
That must be the reason why
I have this desperate desire, this frantic longing

It Was...

It was the way, my naked thigh felt
Pressed against the cool stone wall
That made me love you so

It was the danger of that night
That caused chills to run down my spine
That made my blood heat so

It was the way, you took me with such strength
Under the moon and the bright stars
That made me desire you so

It was the way, my naked thigh felt

Once Again

I find you blanketing the night

I return to you, not scared of your reputation
Instead, I came to unleash your magnificence
Because you are much too glorious to leave unknown
Even as the world becomes docile, your splendor remains
untamed
The silver twinkle of your eyes awakens lost souls
Your fire burns for eternity inside the truth of your fame

I find you blanketing the night

Betrayal

I see clearly now, I see everything,
Once again you betrayed me

I flee to the dark, my only home
The night finds me, with a light breeze that caresses my cheek
Here in the dark all the memories of your betrayal cross my mind
The hurt freezes my soul, not even a single tear falls from my eyes

LEFT ALONE

Everything you did leaves me scarred and jaded
My heart breaks, as your words haunt my every thought
My anger intertwined with hurt, continues to grow with every
waking moment

You've taken over my memories, every beat of my heart.
With every thought, you have darkened my soul.

Just the Thought

Her memories are filled with you
Long black hair spread across her breast

Your hot breath against her neck
With just a look all sadness and anger vanished

A simple touch obliterates all the pain
Flooding her soul in the rush of pleasure

To finally be truly sated and loved with just the thought of you...

She Rose Up

In the center of her garden hidden from the outside world
She rose up out of the emerald green water
Her naked skin glowed in the moonlight

In the center of her garden hidden from the outside world
Long wet red hair flowed down her back
It gleamed and shimmered like silk.

In the center of her garden hidden from the outside world
Tiny drops of water ran along the curves of her breasts
Trailing down her narrow rib cage

In the center of her garden hidden from the outside world
Dipping in at her small waist to skim down her flat belly
Continuing down her long, lean legs

In the center of her gardens hidden from the outside world
She rose up from the emerald green water
Her naked skin glowed in the moonlight

Despite

Do you love me without fear?
Despite our circumstances

Trust me without question?
Despite our disbeliefs

Want me without restriction?
Despite our captivities

Accept me without change?
Despite our differences

Desire me without inhibitions?
Despite our reserves

Will You?

Will you be my mighty king?
If I promise to be the jewel in your crown.

Will you be the wind guiding my wings?
If I promise to never let, you touch the ground.

Will you be the sky so broad and blue?
If I promise to be the cloud at your chest.

Will you be the ocean so deep and pure?
If I promise to be the waves searching for rest.

Will you be the mountain, massive and high?
If I promise to be the green valley so wide.

Will you be my eagle souring in the sky?
If I promise to always fly at your side.

Will you be my mighty king?
If I promise to be the jewel in your crown.

Cold Winter's Night

Waiting on a cold winter's night
Wind blowing through my hair
Standing in the dark, rain freezes on my cheek
Closing my eyes, you run through my mind
Slowly, I breathe in deep and suddenly my life is complete
Only with you, my heart I share
Even though I know you are not there

Waiting on a cold winter's night
Dreaming of lying in your arms
No feeling could ever match
Closing my eyes, you run through my mind
Slowly, I breathe in deep and suddenly my life is complete
Only with you, my soul is left dark
My feelings have never been more concise

Waiting on a cold winter's night
My heart cold as ice…

Amazing News

You expected amazing news
A look at your baby growing in your womb
But before the first look, you got the devastating news
There wasn't a heartbeat and your baby didn't move
Your vision is clouded and your head is confused
Everything is an echo and seems so unreal
Your child is gone and you're left with just tears
Only time is left to heal your broken heart
Your life will continue, but it will never be the same
Because one day you expected amazing news

Background

You're always with us, standing in the background
Waiting for your time, silently watching
Wandering through our darkest thoughts
Even though you come for us all
Your work always seems to surprise
Loathed and feared by most
Occasionally called for by the rest
You're always hiding in the shadows
Taking away all the pain
You come in our dimmest hours
Promising an end to the clouds
You're always with us, standing in the background

www.ingramcontent.com/pod-product-compliance
Lightning Source LLC
Chambersburg PA
CBHW071504070426
42452CB00041B/2291